Whidbey Island Wanderlust: Exploring the Jewel of the Pacific Northwest

"Whidbey Island Wanderlust" invites readers to embark on an immersive journey through the captivating landscapes, rich history, cultural treasures, and hidden gems of this picturesque island in the Pacific Northwest. Whether you're a nature lover, history buff, food enthusiast, or art aficionado, this comprehensive guide offers a vibrant exploration of Whidbey Island's diverse offerings. From breathtaking beaches and scenic trails to charming towns, lively festivals, and a flourishing arts scene, each chapter unravels a new facet of the island's allure, showcasing the experiences that make Whidbey a must-visit destination. Let this book be your compass, inspiring you to embrace the island life, create unforgettable memories, and develop a deep appreciation for the wonders of Whidbey Island.

Table of Contents:

Chapter 1: Introduction to Whidbey Island

Chapter 2: The History and Heritage of Whidbey Island

Chapter 3: Whidbey Island's Natural Splendor: A Visual Delight

Chapter 4: Captivating Beaches: Coastal Charm of Whidbey Island

Chapter 5: Delving into Deception Pass: Nature's Masterpiece

Chapter 6: Island Hopping: Discovering Whidbey's Neighboring Gems

Chapter 7: Whidbey's Wildlife Wonderland: Flora and Fauna Encounters

Chapter 8: Oak Harbor: Gateway to Whidbey Island

Chapter 9: Coupeville: A Charming Seaside Town

Chapter 10: Langley: Art, Culture, and Whimsy

Chapter 11: Exploring Whidbey's Coastal Trails and Parks

Chapter 12: Whidbey's Agricultural Bounty: Farms and Farmers Markets

Chapter 13: Naval Air Station Whidbey Island: A Military Legacy

Chapter 14: Whidbey's Festivals and Events: Celebrations of Island Life

Chapter 15: Island Artistry: Whidbey's Vibrant Arts Scene

Chapter 16: Whidbey's Culinary Delights: A Gastronomic Journey

Chapter 17: Whidbey's Wine and Spirits: A Taste of Local Libations

Chapter 18: Unearthing Whidbey's Hidden Gems: Off-the-Beaten-Path Adventures

Chapter 19: Embracing Island Life: Whidbey's Communities and Residents

Chapter 20: Reflections on Whidbey Island: Fond Farewells and Lasting Memories

Chapter 1: Introduction to Whidbey Island

Welcome to Whidbey Island, a hidden gem nestled in the heart of the Puget Sound, Washington state's emerald playground. This enchanting island, spanning approximately 55 miles in length, captivates visitors with its breathtaking natural beauty, rich history, and vibrant communities. As we embark on this journey, allow me to introduce you to the allure and charm that make Whidbey Island a must-visit destination.

Surrounded by the glistening waters of the Puget Sound and framed by the majestic Olympic and Cascade mountain ranges, Whidbey Island offers a captivating tapestry of landscapes. From rocky shores and sandy beaches to lush forests and rolling farmland, the island's diverse terrain beckons adventurers, nature enthusiasts, and tranquility seekers alike.

Stepping foot on Whidbey Island, you'll be greeted by a sense of calm and serenity. The island's serene atmosphere, coupled with its pristine natural surroundings, provides a much-needed respite from the bustling pace of everyday life. As you traverse the island's scenic roads, you'll encounter picturesque vistas at every turn, inviting you to pause, breathe, and immerse yourself in the tranquility of the moment.

To truly appreciate the island's allure, one must delve into its intriguing history. Whidbey Island has been inhabited by Native American tribes for thousands of years, and their deep connection to the land is still evident today. European explorers and settlers arrived in the 19th century, leaving their mark on the island's development. From tales of early exploration to the establishment of military bases during World War II, Whidbey Island's history is a tapestry woven with stories of resilience, ingenuity, and the enduring spirit of its inhabitants.

As we embark on our exploration, we'll encounter Whidbey Island's vibrant communities, each with its unique character and charm. Oak Harbor, situated on the northern end of the island, welcomes visitors with its bustling waterfront, naval presence, and a vibrant downtown brimming with shops, galleries, and eateries. Coupeville, a charming seaside town with a rich maritime heritage, captivates visitors with its historic buildings, quaint streets, and a vibrant arts scene. The town of Langley, perched on the southern edge of the island, offers a delightful fusion of small-town charm and artistic expression, where galleries, boutiques, and cozy cafes line the streets.

Whidbey Island also boasts an array of outdoor adventures, inviting you to explore its abundant parks, trails, and beaches. From the iconic Deception Pass State Park, with its soaring cliffs and the dramatic Deception Pass Bridge, to the Ebey's Landing National Historical Reserve, a living testament to the island's agricultural heritage and breathtaking coastal views, there's no shortage of opportunities to connect with nature and embark on unforgettable outdoor escapades.

Throughout our journey, we'll savor the island's culinary delights, ranging from farm-fresh produce and locally caught seafood to award-winning wines and craft beverages. Whidbey Island's farm-to-table ethos is showcased in its farmers markets, where you can taste the vibrant flavors of the region and meet the passionate individuals who nurture the land. The island's dining scene offers a delectable fusion of cuisines, with talented chefs crafting culinary masterpieces that highlight the island's bountiful harvest.

As we conclude this introduction to Whidbey Island, let the island's natural beauty, rich history, vibrant communities, and culinary treasures serve as an irresistible invitation to embark on an unforgettable journey. In the chapters to come, we will dive deeper into each facet of this island paradise, unraveling its secrets, and guiding you through the wonders that await your discovery. So, pack your sense of adventure, open your heart to the island's embrace, and prepare to be enchanted by Whidbey Island, the Pacific Northwest's hidden treasure.

In the chapters to come, we will delve into the captivating beaches that adorn Whidbey Island's coastline. From the rugged cliffs of Double Bluff Beach to the sandy shores of Penn Cove, each beach offers its own unique allure. Feel the soft, powdery sand between your toes as you stroll along the shoreline, listen to the rhythmic lapping of waves against the shore, and witness the ever-changing colors of the sky as the sun sets over the water. Whether you seek solitude and reflection or seek adventure in water sports like kayaking and paddleboarding, Whidbey Island's beaches provide the perfect setting for your coastal escape.

One of the island's most iconic landmarks, Deception Pass, awaits our exploration. As we traverse the Deception Pass Bridge, a marvel of engineering that connects Whidbey Island to Fidalgo Island, we'll be greeted by breathtaking views of turbulent waters rushing through the narrow strait. Hiking trails meander through the surrounding state park, offering panoramic vistas and the chance to witness the raw power of nature up close.

But Whidbey Island's wonders extend beyond its shores. Just a short ferry ride away lie neighboring islands like Camano Island and the San Juan Islands, each with its own distinct charm and natural splendor. Embarking on an island-hopping adventure allows you to explore hidden coves, encounter diverse wildlife, and embrace the tranquility that comes with island living.

Nature enthusiasts will find themselves in paradise as they discover Whidbey Island's wildlife wonders. From birdwatching at Crockett Lake or the Admiralty Inlet Preserve to spotting seals, sea lions, and even orcas along the coast, the island's diverse ecosystems provide a sanctuary for a rich array of fauna. Keep your camera at the ready, as you never know when you might encounter a majestic bald eagle soaring overhead or a deer gracefully traversing the forest trails.

While Whidbey Island's natural beauty is undeniably captivating, its towns and communities add a touch of charm and warmth to the island's character. Oak Harbor, the largest city on the island, offers a vibrant blend of maritime heritage and modern amenities. Explore the Naval Air Station Whidbey Island, home to impressive aircraft displays and a testament to the island's military legacy. Engage in the local art scene, browse unique shops, and savor the flavors of the Pacific Northwest at cozy cafes and restaurants.

Coupeville, one of the oldest towns in Washington state, exudes a timeless coastal ambiance. Its historic waterfront beckons with its Victorian-era buildings, waterfront parks, and the Coupeville Wharf. Take a leisurely stroll along the pier, savor freshly caught seafood, and immerse yourself in the town's seafaring history. Don't miss the annual Penn

Cove Mussel Festival, a celebration of the island's prized bivalve and a testament to the close-knit community spirit.

As our journey continues, we'll make our way to Langley, a captivating town known for its vibrant arts scene and scenic vistas. Perched on a bluff overlooking Saratoga Passage, Langley invites visitors to explore its art galleries, boutique shops, and charming streets. Attend a live performance at the Whidbey Island Center for the Arts or indulge in culinary delights at one of the town's acclaimed restaurants. Langley's picturesque beauty and creative energy make it a destination that nourishes both the soul and the senses.

Whidbey Island's natural abundance is reflected in its numerous parks and trails that beckon adventurers and outdoor enthusiasts. Lace up your hiking boots and traverse the scenic trails of South Whidbey State Park, where moss-covered forests, cascading waterfalls, and serene lakes await. Ebey's Landing National Historical Reserve offers a unique blend of history and nature, with its well-preserved farmland, coastal bluffs, and sweeping views of Admiralty Inlet.

As we meander through the chapters of our journey, we'll uncover the island's agricultural bounty. Whidbey Island's fertile soil and mild climate create an ideal environment for a thriving agricultural community. Local farms and farmers markets offer an abundance of fresh produce, artisanal goods, and the opportunity to connect with the passionate individuals who cultivate the land. Savor the flavors of farm-to-table cuisine, sample artisan cheeses, and delight in the vibrant colors and aromas of the island's agricultural tapestry.

With its rich history, Whidbey Island has stories to tell. The Naval Air Station Whidbey Island stands as a testament to the island's military heritage and serves as a base for naval aviation operations. Explore the museum, gain insight into the island's role in defending the nation, and witness the awe-inspiring power of aircraft taking flight.

Throughout the year, Whidbey Island comes alive with festivals and events that celebrate the island's unique culture and community spirit. From the Whidbey Island Highland Games, where bagpipes echo through the air and athletic feats impress spectators, to the Penn Cove Water Festival, a celebration of Native American traditions and the island's maritime history, these events provide a vibrant tapestry of experiences that showcase the island's lively spirit.

As we immerse ourselves in Whidbey Island's art scene, we'll discover a flourishing community of artists, artisans, and performers. The island's galleries, studios, and theaters offer a diverse range of artistic expressions, from painting and sculpture to theater and music. Engage with local artists, attend gallery openings and live performances, and witness firsthand the creative energy that permeates the island.

No exploration of Whidbey Island would be complete without indulging in its culinary delights. Whidbey's chefs, bakers, and vintners take advantage of the island's natural bounty, crafting exceptional dishes and libations. Savor the flavors of locally sourced seafood, delight in farm-fresh produce, and embark on a wine-tasting adventure at one of the island's esteemed wineries. Whidbey Island offers a delectable culinary landscape that tempts and delights every palate.

As we navigate off the beaten path, we'll uncover hidden gems that showcase the island's unique character. From tucked-away cafes and charming bed and breakfasts to secret beaches and lesser-known hiking trails, these discoveries provide intimate and unforgettable experiences for the intrepid traveler.

Whidbey Island's communities and residents are the heart and soul of the island's identity. Engage with locals, hear their stories, and embrace the warm hospitality that makes Whidbey Island a welcoming destination. Whether it's participating in community events, exploring the island's lively markets, or simply striking up a conversation with a friendly face, the island's sense of community invites you to become a part of its tapestry.

As our journey draws to a close, take a moment to reflect on the memories forged on Whidbey Island. From the awe-inspiring landscapes and rich history to the vibrant communities and culinary delights, this island paradise leaves an indelible mark on all who visit. May your time on Whidbey Island be filled with enchantment, discovery, and a deep appreciation for the wonders of this Pacific Northwest gem.

So, let us embark on this extraordinary adventure through Whidbey Island, where natural beauty, captivating history, and vibrant communities intertwine to create an experience that will linger in your heart long after you depart its shores. Welcome to Whidbey Island, where dreams are awakened, and the spirit of exploration comes alive.

Chapter 2: The History and Heritage of Whidbey Island

Whidbey Island is steeped in a rich tapestry of history and heritage, woven together by the stories of its indigenous people, early explorers, settlers, and the resilient communities that have shaped its identity over the centuries. In this chapter, we delve into the island's past, unraveling its historical significance and exploring the heritage that continues to thrive today.

Long before European explorers arrived, Whidbey Island was inhabited by the indigenous Coast Salish people, particularly the Snohomish, Skagit, and Swinomish tribes. For thousands of years, these Native American communities lived in harmony with the land and sea, relying on its abundant resources for sustenance and cultural expression. Their deep connection to the island's natural surroundings is still evident in their traditions, art, and oral histories passed down through generations.

European exploration of the Pacific Northwest brought the first outsiders to Whidbey Island's shores. In 1792, Captain George Vancouver, an officer in the British Royal Navy, charted the waters of the Puget Sound and discovered the island that would later bear the name of his colleague, Joseph Whidbey. Vancouver's expedition, part of a larger effort to map the region, marked the beginning of European influence on the island.

In the early 19th century, American and British fur traders established trading posts in the region, interacting with the native populations and creating a cultural exchange that would shape the island's history. The Hudson's Bay Company, a British fur trading company, played a significant role in the economic and social development of the Pacific Northwest, including Whidbey Island.

The mid-1800s brought a wave of settlers to the island, primarily attracted by the fertile soil, abundance of timber, and opportunities for agriculture. These pioneers, many of whom were of European descent, built farms and established communities that would become the foundation of Whidbey Island's heritage. Towns like Coupeville and Langley emerged as trading hubs, serving as gateways to the island's resources and linking it to the broader Puget Sound region.

Whidbey Island's strategic location made it a vital military outpost during times of conflict. During World War II, the U.S. Navy established Naval Air Station Whidbey Island, which continues to operate today. The naval base has been a significant presence on the island, shaping its economy and fostering a strong connection between the military and civilian communities. Visitors can explore the base's museum, learn about its history, and witness the impressive aircraft that take flight from its runways.

As you journey through Whidbey Island, traces of its past can be found in the historic buildings, landmarks, and cultural institutions that tell the stories of those who came before. The Coupeville Wharf, built in 1905, is a living testament to the island's maritime heritage and offers a glimpse into its early days as a bustling port. Ebey's Landing National Historical Reserve, a designated historical district, preserves the island's rural character and showcases the well-preserved farmsteads and structures that harken back to a bygone era.

Preservation of Whidbey Island's historical and cultural heritage is a shared commitment among its residents and organizations. Museums, such as the Island County Historical Society Museum in Coupeville, provide a deeper understanding of the island's past through exhibits, artifacts, and educational programs. The preservation of Native American culture and history is also honored through collaborations with indigenous communities, ensuring that their voices are heard and their traditions are respected.

The traditions of Whidbey Island's past are not only celebrated but also integrated into the fabric of daily life. Festivals and events pay homage to the island's history, allowing visitors to engage in living history experiences. The

Loganberry Festival in Greenbank, for example, commemorates the island's agricultural heritage, showcasing the iconic Loganberry fruit that was cultivated on the island in the early 20th century.

Whidbey Island's history and heritage are not confined to the pages of books or the walls of museums; they are alive and thriving within its communities. The island's residents take pride in their heritage, honoring their ancestors and preserving the traditions that have shaped their way of life. From storytelling and traditional crafts to music and dance, the cultural vitality of Whidbey Island is a testament to the enduring legacy of its past.

As you explore Whidbey Island, take the time to immerse yourself in its history and heritage. Engage with the local community, visit historical sites and museums, and listen to the stories passed down through generations. By understanding the island's past, you gain a deeper appreciation for its present and a greater sense of connection to the land, the people, and the vibrant tapestry that is Whidbey Island.

Chapter 3: Whidbey Island's Natural Splendor: A Visual Delight

Whidbey Island is a haven of natural splendor, a place where breathtaking landscapes and diverse ecosystems converge to create a visual feast for the senses. In this chapter, we embark on a journey through the island's remarkable natural beauty, exploring its pristine forests, cascading waterfalls, picturesque lakes, and awe-inspiring vistas.

The island's scenic allure begins with its coastline, where rocky shores, sandy beaches, and towering bluffs coexist harmoniously. As you wander along the beaches, you'll be captivated by the rhythm of the waves, the salty sea breeze caressing your skin, and the expansive views of the surrounding waters. Double Bluff Beach, with its dramatic cliffs and panoramic views, is a perfect spot for contemplation, while the serene sandy expanses of Ebey's Landing provide tranquility and an opportunity to observe shorebirds in their natural habitat.

Inland, Whidbey Island reveals a diverse array of natural wonders. Exploring the island's forests, you'll find yourself surrounded by towering trees, moss-covered branches, and the earthy scent of the undergrowth. South Whidbey State Park, nestled within a dense forested area, offers an extensive trail system where you can immerse yourself in the beauty of the island's lush woodlands. Let the sunlight filter through the canopy as you hike, and listen to the melodic symphony of birdsong that fills the air.

Waterfalls cascade down rocky cliffs, adding a touch of magic to the island's landscapes. The enchanting waterfall at Saratoga Woods, hidden within a mossy forest, creates a serene and captivating atmosphere, inviting you to pause and appreciate the raw power and beauty of nature. The sound of rushing water and the shimmering cascade evoke a sense of tranquility and awe.

Whidbey Island's lakes and wetlands provide a sanctuary for a diverse array of wildlife and offer serene spots for reflection. Goss Lake, with its still waters reflecting the surrounding forests, is a haven for birdwatchers and kayakers alike. Watch as herons gracefully wade in the shallows, or glide across the lake's surface, immersing yourself in the serenity of this hidden gem.

One of the island's most iconic natural features is Deception Pass, a strait that separates Whidbey Island from Fidalgo Island. The Deception Pass Bridge, an engineering marvel, spans the turbulent waters below and offers breathtaking views of swirling currents, rugged cliffs, and distant islands. Standing atop the bridge, you'll feel a sense of awe as you witness the sheer power and beauty of this natural phenomenon.

Venturing further into Whidbey Island's interior, you'll discover its rolling farmlands and vineyards. Embrace the pastoral beauty of the countryside, where fields of vibrant crops stretch towards the horizon. Visit local farms and experience the joy of picking fresh berries or sampling artisanal cheeses made from the milk of contented cows grazing on lush pastures. Whidbey Island's agricultural heritage is alive and well, and a visit to one of the many farms offers a glimpse into a simpler way of life and a connection to the land.

From the verdant forests to the breathtaking coastlines, Whidbey Island's natural splendor is a visual delight that invites you to reconnect with the wonders of the natural world. As you explore the island's landscapes, take the time to breathe in the crisp air, listen to the whispers of the wind, and marvel at the ever-changing tableau that unfolds before your eyes. Whidbey Island is a sanctuary of beauty, a place where the interplay of land, sea, and sky creates a visual symphony that will leave an indelible impression on your heart.

Chapter 4: Captivating Beaches: Coastal Charm of Whidbey Island

Whidbey Island's coastline is adorned with a collection of captivating beaches, each with its own unique charm and allure. In this chapter, we embark on a journey along the sandy shores and rocky cliffs, discovering the beauty and serenity of Whidbey Island's coastal treasures.

Double Bluff Beach, located on the southwestern edge of the island, is a hidden gem that showcases the rugged beauty of Whidbey's shoreline. As you walk along the sandy expanse, you'll be greeted by towering bluffs and dramatic cliffs that rise majestically from the sea. The panoramic views of the Strait of Juan de Fuca and the Olympic Mountains in the distance create a mesmerizing backdrop for your beachside adventures. Explore tide pools teeming with marine life, watch for eagles soaring overhead, and revel in the tranquility that envelops this secluded stretch of coastline.

Penn Cove, nestled on the eastern side of Whidbey Island, is known for its tranquil waters and picturesque charm. This idyllic bay is a haven for boating enthusiasts and offers opportunities for kayaking, paddleboarding, and sailing. Stroll along the sandy beach, enjoy a picnic with panoramic views, or embark on a wildlife-watching excursion. Keep an eye out for the resident pod of orcas that occasionally graces these waters, delighting visitors with their graceful presence.

Langley's Seawall Park, with its waterfront promenade, invites you to unwind and soak in the coastal ambiance. As you walk along the wooden boardwalk, take in the views of Saratoga Passage and the Cascade Mountains, and feel the gentle sea breeze caress your skin. This charming park is also a prime spot for spotting gray whales during their migration season. Marvel at these majestic creatures as they journey through the waters, adding a touch of wonder to your coastal experience.

On the northern end of the island, Joseph Whidbey State Park beckons with its natural beauty and tranquil atmosphere. This expansive beach offers a peaceful retreat, where you can stroll along the shoreline, collect seashells, and enjoy uninterrupted views of the water. With its scenic picnic areas and abundant birdlife, Joseph Whidbey State Park provides a serene escape from the bustle of daily life.

Deception Pass State Park, a crown jewel of Whidbey Island, offers an immersive coastal experience that will leave you in awe. The park's namesake, Deception Pass, is a dramatic strait where powerful tidal currents rush through a narrow channel, creating a spectacle of natural forces. Walk across the iconic Deception Pass Bridge and witness the swirling waters below, or venture down to the beaches to explore the rocky coves and tide pools. With its extensive trail system, the park invites hikers to meander through old-growth forests, providing glimpses of the rugged coastline and breathtaking vistas along the way.

As you traverse Whidbey Island's beaches, remember to tread lightly and respect the fragile coastal ecosystem. Take care to leave no trace, preserving the pristine beauty for future generations to enjoy. Whether you seek solitude, adventure, or simply a place to connect with the rhythm of the sea, Whidbey Island's captivating beaches offer a coastal escape that will soothe your soul and leave you with lasting memories of this coastal paradise.

Chapter 5: Delving into Deception Pass: Nature's Masterpiece

Deception Pass, a breathtaking natural wonder that connects Whidbey Island to Fidalgo Island, deserves its own chapter of exploration. In Chapter 5, we delve into the splendor of Deception Pass State Park and its iconic bridge, immersing ourselves in the raw beauty and captivating landscapes that make it a true masterpiece of nature.

Deception Pass State Park encompasses over 3,800 acres of diverse landscapes, including old-growth forests, rocky cliffs, and pristine beaches. As you step foot into this magnificent park, you'll immediately feel a sense of awe and wonder. Towering evergreen trees, their branches adorned with moss and ferns, create a serene canopy overhead, while sunlight filters through, casting ethereal patterns on the forest floor.

The heart of Deception Pass State Park is undoubtedly the Deception Pass Bridge. This iconic steel bridge, towering high above the swirling waters of the pass, serves as a gateway to adventure and a testament to human engineering. As you walk across the bridge or stand at one of its viewpoints, the views that unfold before you are nothing short of spectacular. The turquoise waters of Deception Pass, framed by rocky cliffs and forested islands, captivate the senses and stir the imagination. Watch as the tidal currents rush through the narrow strait, creating whirlpools and eddies that dance in a mesmerizing display of natural power.

To truly appreciate the park's wonders, venture down to its beaches and coves. Bowman Bay, nestled within the park, offers a tranquil setting with a sandy beach and calm waters, perfect for swimming, picnicking, and beachcombing. Explore the tide pools teeming with vibrant sea life, or launch a kayak to paddle along the shoreline, admiring the rugged cliffs and hidden alcoves.

If you're feeling adventurous, embark on one of the park's hiking trails to discover hidden gems and breathtaking vistas. The Goose Rock Trail, a moderate hike, takes you to the highest point on Whidbey Island, rewarding you with panoramic views of the surrounding landscape. The Lottie Bay Trail meanders through lush forests and leads you to a secluded beach, where you can bask in the tranquility of the surroundings. Along the way, keep an eye out for diverse wildlife, including deer, eagles, and a variety of bird species.

For those seeking an adrenaline rush, consider rock climbing or bouldering at the park's designated climbing area. With its sheer cliffs and challenging routes, Deception Pass offers a thrilling playground for climbers of all levels. Feel the exhilaration as you ascend the rugged rock faces and savor the stunning views from your elevated vantage point.

As you explore Deception Pass State Park, take a moment to appreciate its ecological significance. The park is not only a haven for outdoor enthusiasts but also a sanctuary for a diverse array of plant and animal species. Coastal forests, saltwater marshes, and intertidal zones support a rich ecosystem, providing habitat for native flora and fauna. Keep your eyes peeled for sightings of seabirds, seals, and even occasional glimpses of orcas that frequent these waters.

Whether you choose to stroll along the beaches, hike through the forested trails, or simply sit in quiet contemplation, Deception Pass offers an immersive experience with nature that will rejuvenate your spirit and leave you with a profound connection to the natural world.

As you bid farewell to Deception Pass and its majestic beauty, remember the sense of wonder and awe it has instilled within you. This masterpiece of nature serves as a reminder of the Earth's immense power and beauty, urging us to preserve and protect such treasures for generations to come. Whidbey Island's Deception Pass State Park stands as a testament to the magnificence of the natural world and invites you to immerse yourself in its splendor.

Chapter 6: Island Hopping: Discovering Whidbey's Neighboring Gems

Whidbey Island, with its captivating beauty, serves as a gateway to a cluster of neighboring gems scattered throughout the surrounding waters. In Chapter 6, we embark on an island-hopping adventure, exploring the unique charms and natural wonders of these nearby islands that complement Whidbey's allure.

Camano Island, located just a short distance to the east, is an idyllic retreat that enchants visitors with its laid-back atmosphere and natural splendor. Accessible by bridge, Camano Island boasts pristine beaches, serene woodlands, and panoramic views of the surrounding waters. Explore Cama Beach State Park, where you can hike the forested trails, relax on the sandy shores, or rent a kayak to paddle along the calm waters of Saratoga Passage. Don't miss the opportunity to visit the Camano Island State Park, known for its tranquil beauty and abundant wildlife, including bald eagles, herons, and even occasional sightings of gray whales.

The San Juan Islands, an archipelago situated to the northwest of Whidbey Island, offer a collection of picturesque islands known for their unspoiled landscapes and charming communities. Orcas Island, the largest of the San Juans, captivates visitors with its stunning beauty and diverse ecosystems. Embark on a hike up Mount Constitution, the highest point in the islands, and be rewarded with panoramic views that stretch across the surrounding islands and beyond. Enjoy the vibrant arts scene and browse the unique shops in the quaint village of Eastsound.

Lopez Island, the third largest of the San Juans, is a tranquil oasis of pastoral beauty and welcoming communities. Known for its rolling farmland and meandering country roads, Lopez Island invites visitors to slow down and embrace the simple pleasures of island life. Rent a bicycle and pedal along scenic routes, passing by picturesque farms, vineyards, and stunning coastal views. Delight in the island's farm-to-table cuisine, with several farm stands and local eateries offering delectable treats made from the island's bountiful harvest.

Shaw Island, one of the lesser-known San Juan Islands, offers a serene and off-the-beaten-path experience. The island is primarily residential, with a small population and limited tourist amenities. This peaceful retreat provides an opportunity to disconnect from the outside world and immerse yourself in nature's tranquility. Explore the shoreline, go beachcombing, or take a leisurely stroll along the quiet country roads that wind through the island's interior.

As you island-hop through these neighboring gems, embrace the unique character and natural beauty that each has to offer. Immerse yourself in the slower pace of island life, savor the stunning vistas, and engage with the friendly communities that call these islands home.

Back on Whidbey Island, reflect on the experiences and memories forged during your island-hopping adventure. The proximity of these neighboring gems adds another layer of exploration to your Whidbey journey, expanding your horizons and deepening your appreciation for the Pacific Northwest's island treasures.

Whether you choose to embark on a day trip or spend a few nights immersing yourself in the island lifestyle, the neighboring gems surrounding Whidbey Island provide a delightful extension to your coastal adventure. Embrace the enchantment of island hopping and discover the hidden treasures that await on these idyllic isles, creating a truly unforgettable experience.

Chapter 7: Whidbey's Wildlife Wonderland: Flora and Fauna Encounters

Whidbey Island is a wildlife wonderland, where diverse ecosystems and pristine habitats provide a sanctuary for a wide array of flora and fauna. In Chapter 7, we embark on a journey through the island's natural landscapes, immersing ourselves in the captivating encounters with the island's wildlife.

As we delve into Whidbey Island's wilderness, we'll encounter a rich variety of bird species that call the island home. From majestic bald eagles soaring through the skies to the melodic calls of songbirds hidden among the trees, the avian inhabitants of Whidbey Island provide a symphony of sights and sounds. Keep your binoculars at the ready as you traverse the trails of South Whidbey State Park or venture to the wetlands of Crockett Lake. Observe herons gracefully wading in the shallows, listen to the distinctive call of the elusive Pacific-slope flycatcher, or witness the sight of a great blue heron taking flight from the water's edge.

Whidbey Island's coastal proximity offers a unique opportunity to spot marine life along its shores. Seals and sea lions can often be seen basking on the rocky outcroppings or swimming playfully in the waves. If you're fortunate, you may even witness pods of orcas passing through the waters during their seasonal migrations, a truly awe-inspiring sight. Join a whale-watching tour or find a vantage point along the beach, and be prepared to be mesmerized by these magnificent creatures as they navigate the sea.

The island's forests and meadows are also home to an abundance of land-dwelling animals. As you wander through the woodlands, keep an eye out for deer gracefully traversing the undergrowth, their gentle presence adding to the tranquility of the surroundings. Coyotes, raccoons, and foxes may make appearances in the early morning or evening hours, stealthily exploring their territories. Patient observers may even catch glimpses of elusive creatures such as bobcats or black bears, which roam the island's wilderness.

Whidbey Island's diverse ecosystems create a haven for a myriad of plant species, each contributing to the island's natural beauty. Explore the moss-draped forests, where towering Douglas firs, Western red cedars, and Western hemlocks create a verdant canopy overhead. Wander through fields adorned with wildflowers, such as lupines, camas, and Indian paintbrush, adding vibrant splashes of color to the landscape. Take in the sweet fragrance of the wild roses that bloom along the coastline, their delicate petals embracing the salty breeze.

Engage in the island's commitment to conservation and education by visiting organizations dedicated to preserving and protecting the island's wildlife and ecosystems. The Admiralty Audubon Society and Whidbey Camano Land Trust offer programs and events that allow visitors to deepen their understanding of the island's flora and fauna. Participate in birdwatching excursions, guided hikes, and educational workshops to further enrich your wildlife encounters.

As you journey through Whidbey Island's wildlife wonderland, remember to tread lightly and respect the natural habitats of the island's residents. Admire from a distance, allowing animals to maintain their natural behaviors and undisturbed habitats. Take only photographs and memories, leaving no trace behind. By fostering a deep appreciation for Whidbey's diverse flora and fauna, we contribute to the preservation of this island paradise for generations to come.

Whidbey Island's wildlife encounters offer a glimpse into the intricate tapestry of the natural world. Whether observing soaring eagles, listening to the melodies of songbirds, or witnessing the marine wonders of the sea, these encounters remind us of the interconnectedness and beauty of all living beings. Embrace the magic of Whidbey's wildlife wonderland and let the island's captivating creatures leave an indelible mark on your heart and soul.

Chapter 8: Whidbey Island's Culinary Delights: A Taste of the Pacific Northwest

Whidbey Island's culinary scene is a tantalizing tapestry of flavors, drawing inspiration from the bountiful harvests of the Pacific Northwest. In Chapter 8, we embark on a culinary journey, savoring the island's delectable delights and discovering the unique tastes that make Whidbey a food lover's paradise.

Farm-to-table is more than just a trend on Whidbey Island; it's a way of life. The island's fertile soil and temperate climate create an ideal environment for sustainable agriculture, resulting in a vibrant local food culture. As you explore the island, visit one of the many farmers markets, where you'll find an abundance of fresh produce, artisanal goods, and the opportunity to meet the passionate individuals who cultivate the land. Taste the sweetness of freshly picked berries, sample the crispness of just-harvested vegetables, and indulge in the creaminess of locally made cheeses.

Whidbey Island's connection to the sea is evident in its thriving seafood scene. From succulent Dungeness crab and plump Penn Cove mussels to perfectly grilled salmon, the island's coastal waters provide a rich bounty of delicacies. Visit one of the local seafood markets or dine at waterfront restaurants to savor the ocean's treasures. Treat yourself to a classic seafood boil, where you can feast on a medley of shellfish, corn, and potatoes, or indulge in a bowl of creamy seafood chowder, brimming with the flavors of the sea.

For wine enthusiasts, Whidbey Island boasts a flourishing wine industry. The island's unique microclimate, combined with its fertile soil, produces grapes that result in exceptional wines. Embark on a wine-tasting adventure at one of the island's acclaimed wineries, where you can sample a variety of varietals, from crisp whites to robust reds. Engage with the passionate winemakers, learn about their craft, and toast to the flavors of the Pacific Northwest.

Whidbey Island's culinary scene extends beyond farm-fresh produce and seafood. The island's charming towns are home to a vibrant array of restaurants, cafes, and bakeries that showcase the talents of local chefs and artisans. Indulge in a gourmet meal crafted from locally sourced ingredients, where every bite tells a story of the region's rich agricultural heritage. Savor the flavors of Northwest cuisine, characterized by its emphasis on fresh, seasonal ingredients and creative culinary techniques.

As you traverse Whidbey Island, be sure to explore the unique experiences that the island's culinary scene has to offer. Join a cooking class where you can learn to prepare

Pacific Northwest-inspired dishes, participate in a farm-to-table feast that highlights the island's local ingredients, or attend one of the island's many food festivals and events, where you can sample a wide range of culinary delights.

Whidbey Island's culinary treasures extend beyond the plate. The island's sense of community and passion for food is evident in the many food-related events and gatherings that bring locals and visitors together. From the Penn Cove Mussel Festival, a celebration of the island's prized bivalve, to the Harvest Festivals that mark the changing seasons, these events showcase the island's rich culinary heritage and the vibrant spirit of its inhabitants.

As you conclude your culinary journey on Whidbey Island, take a moment to savor the flavors and appreciate the connections forged between the land, the sea, and the community. Whidbey's culinary delights invite you to indulge in the tastes of the Pacific Northwest, to experience the essence of the island through its vibrant flavors, and to create lasting memories around the table. So, raise your glass, take a bite, and let Whidbey Island's culinary treasures awaken your senses and nourish your soul.

Chapter 9: Charming Communities: Embracing Whidbey Island's Towns and Villages

Whidbey Island is not only a place of natural beauty but also a tapestry of charming communities that add a touch of warmth and character to the island's identity. In Chapter 9, we delve into the distinct qualities of Whidbey's towns and villages, immersing ourselves in their unique atmospheres and discovering the hidden gems that make each community special.

Oak Harbor, the largest city on Whidbey Island, embodies a vibrant blend of maritime heritage and modern amenities. As you stroll through the downtown core, you'll be greeted by a lively atmosphere, where a mix of local boutiques, art galleries, and charming cafes beckon with their enticing offerings. Explore the Oak Harbor Farmers Market, where you can taste the flavors of the island, or visit the PBY-Naval Air Museum to delve into the island's military history. With its scenic waterfront and views of Penn Cove, Oak Harbor provides a perfect blend of urban conveniences and coastal charm.

Coupeville, one of the oldest towns in Washington state, exudes a timeless coastal ambiance that transports visitors to a bygone era. Its historic waterfront, lined with Victorian-era buildings, invites leisurely strolls along the pier, where the salty sea breeze mingles with the scents of freshly caught seafood. Immerse yourself in the town's seafaring history at the Coupeville Wharf, where you can watch fishing boats return with their daily catch or even try your hand at crabbing from the pier. The annual Penn Cove Mussel Festival, a celebration of the island's prized bivalve, showcases Coupeville's close-knit community spirit and offers a taste of its culinary prowess.

Langley, perched on a bluff overlooking Saratoga Passage, captivates visitors with its artistic energy and picturesque beauty. This vibrant town boasts a lively arts scene, with numerous galleries and studios showcasing the works of local artists. Explore the charming streets lined with boutique shops, cozy cafes, and restaurants that specialize in farm-to-table cuisine. Attend a live performance at the Whidbey Island Center for the Arts, where you can immerse yourself in the island's vibrant cultural scene. Langley's breathtaking views of the water and its creative spirit make it a destination that nourishes both the soul and the senses.

Clinton, the gateway to Whidbey Island, is a quaint village that welcomes visitors with its small-town charm. Located near the Clinton Ferry Terminal, this community offers a range of amenities for travelers and locals alike. Explore the small shops and cafes along the main street, or embark on a beach walk to enjoy views of the ferry traffic and the surrounding waters. Clinton is a perfect starting point for your Whidbey Island adventure, serving as a warm introduction to the island's wonders.

Each community on Whidbey Island has its own story to tell and its own unique character. Engage with the locals, immerse yourself in the vibrant energy of the towns, and let their warm hospitality envelop you. Whether it's attending community events, exploring local markets, or simply striking up a conversation with a friendly face, the towns and villages of Whidbey Island invite you to become a part of their tapestry.

As you conclude your exploration of Whidbey Island's communities, reflect on the connections forged and the memories created. The island's towns and villages, with their distinct qualities and welcoming spirit, add depth and richness to the island's allure. Embrace the sense of community, celebrate the island's history and heritage, and appreciate the unique charm that each town brings to the island's mosaic. Whidbey Island's communities are not just places to visit but places to belong, creating a sense of home away from home.

Chapter 10: Arts and Culture: Whidbey Island's Creative Expression

Whidbey Island is a haven for artists, artisans, and performers, who infuse the island with a vibrant creative energy. In Chapter 10, we delve into the arts and culture scene of Whidbey Island, immersing ourselves in the diverse expressions of creativity that make the island a hub for artistic inspiration.

The arts scene on Whidbey Island is as varied as it is vibrant. Galleries and studios dot the island, showcasing an eclectic range of artistic mediums, from painting and sculpture to ceramics and glasswork. Langley, in particular, is known for its thriving arts community, with numerous galleries lining the streets. Wander through these artistic spaces, allowing your senses to be awakened by the colors, textures, and stories conveyed by the works of local artists. Engage with the artists themselves, gaining insights into their creative process and the inspiration they draw from the island's natural beauty.

The performing arts flourish on Whidbey Island, captivating audiences with a variety of theatrical productions, music performances, and dance shows. The Whidbey Island Center for the Arts in Langley is a cultural hub, hosting a diverse range of performances throughout the year. From thought-provoking plays and musicals to captivating concerts and dance recitals, the stage comes alive with talent and creativity. Attend a live performance and let the energy of the performers and the passion of the audience transport you to new emotional heights.

Whidbey Island's artistic expression extends beyond galleries and theaters. The island is home to numerous festivals and events that celebrate the arts and showcase the island's creative spirit. The Whidbey Island Open Studio Tour invites visitors to explore the working spaces of local artists, providing a behind-the-scenes glimpse into their artistic process. The Whidbey Island Film Festival screens independent films that spark conversations and inspire dialogue. From poetry readings to art walks, these events offer opportunities to engage with the island's artistic community and discover new forms of creative expression.

The island's creative vitality is not limited to established artists. Whidbey Island fosters an environment that encourages individuals of all ages to embrace their own creative journeys. Take part in a painting workshop, learn the intricacies of pottery, or join a writing group to nurture your own artistic voice. Whidbey Island is a place where creativity is celebrated and nurtured, offering opportunities for both seasoned artists and those discovering their artistic passion.

The natural beauty and tranquil landscapes of Whidbey Island provide an endless source of inspiration for artists. The interplay of light and shadow, the vivid colors of the sky at sunset, and the ever-changing textures of the coastline are all reflected in the artwork created on the island. As you immerse yourself in the arts and culture of Whidbey Island, you'll gain a deeper appreciation for the profound connection between art and the natural world.

Take a piece of Whidbey Island's creative spirit home with you by visiting the island's galleries and studios, attending performances and events, and engaging with the local artistic community. Let the artistic expression of Whidbey Island ignite your own creative spark, allowing you to see the world through a new lens and embrace the beauty of creative exploration.

In concluding your exploration of Whidbey Island's arts and culture scene, reflect on the power of artistic expression to transcend boundaries and enrich our lives. Whidbey Island's creative community is a testament to the transformative power of art, reminding us of the beauty and inspiration that can be found in every corner of the island.

Chapter 11: Outdoor Adventures: Embrace Whidbey Island's Natural Playground

Whidbey Island's natural playground beckons outdoor enthusiasts with a plethora of thrilling adventures and recreational opportunities. In Chapter 11, we dive into the island's outdoor offerings, embracing the spirit of adventure and exploring the diverse landscapes that make Whidbey a paradise for outdoor lovers.

Hiking trails crisscross Whidbey Island, leading adventurers through a tapestry of natural wonders. From gentle strolls to challenging treks, there is a trail for every level of hiker. Explore the dense forests of South Whidbey State Park, where moss-covered trees create a magical ambiance, or wander along the bluffs of Ebey's Landing National Historical Reserve, with breathtaking views of the coastline. The Kettles Trail in Coupeville takes you through a geological wonderland, showcasing the island's unique glacial history. Lace up your hiking boots, breathe in the fresh air, and let the trails of Whidbey Island lead you to hidden gems and stunning vistas.

Whidbey Island's coastline offers endless opportunities for water-based adventures. Kayak along the rugged shorelines, exploring hidden coves and sea caves. Paddleboarding allows you to glide across the calm waters, providing a unique perspective of the island's coastal beauty. For thrill-seekers, try your hand at kiteboarding or windsurfing, harnessing the power of the wind as you ride the waves. Whidbey Island's proximity to the Puget Sound and its surrounding waters makes it a playground for aquatic adventurers.

The island's beaches provide more than just a place to soak up the sun. Embark on a beachcombing adventure, combing the shores for treasures washed up by the tides. Search for agates, seashells, and other fascinating finds as you embrace the tranquility of the coastline. Many of the beaches are also ideal for picnicking, building sandcastles, or simply basking in the beauty of the ocean's expanse. From Double Bluff Beach to Penn Cove, the island's sandy shores offer a place to relax and rejuvenate.

Whidbey Island's abundant waterways provide excellent opportunities for fishing and crabbing. Cast a line from the shoreline or embark on a fishing charter to explore the deeper waters. Whidbey Island's waters are teeming with salmon, trout, and a variety of other fish species, making it a paradise for anglers. Crabbing is another popular activity, with the island's many piers and marinas providing easy access to prime crabbing spots. Drop your crab pots and savor the thrill of pulling up a delicious Dungeness crab.

For those seeking a bird's-eye view of the island's beauty, consider taking a scenic flight or hot air balloon ride. Soar above Whidbey Island's landscapes, marveling at the lush forests, sparkling waters, and patchwork farmlands below. Capture breathtaking aerial photographs that encapsulate the island's natural splendor.

Whidbey Island's natural playground invites outdoor enthusiasts of all ages and skill levels to embrace the spirit of adventure and connect with the island's natural wonders. Whether hiking through the forests, exploring the coastlines, or engaging in water-based activities, the outdoor offerings of Whidbey Island create memories that will last a lifetime. So, dive in, lace up, paddle out, and let the island's natural playground become your ultimate outdoor sanctuary.

As you reflect on your outdoor adventures on Whidbey Island, appreciate the island's commitment to preserving its natural beauty. Leave no trace, respect wildlife and their habitats, and engage with the local community to learn about conservation efforts. Whidbey Island's natural playground is a precious gift, and by embracing responsible outdoor practices, we ensure that future generations can continue to enjoy its wonders.

Chapter 12: Events and Festivals: Celebrating Whidbey Island's Vibrant Spirit

Whidbey Island's vibrant spirit is celebrated through a calendar filled with lively events and festivals that showcase the island's rich culture and community. In Chapter 12, we immerse ourselves in the excitement of these gatherings, joining in the revelry and discovering the unique traditions that make Whidbey Island come alive.

The Penn Cove Mussel Festival, held in Coupeville each spring, is a beloved event that pays homage to the island's prized bivalve. This festive celebration features mouthwatering seafood dishes, cooking demonstrations, live music, and art exhibits. Join in the mussel chowder tasting competition, sample locally harvested mussels, and delight in the lively atmosphere as the community comes together to honor this culinary treasure.

Whidbey Island is no stranger to the arts, and the Whidbey Island Open Studio Tour provides an opportunity to engage with the island's thriving creative community. This self-guided tour takes visitors into the private studios of local artists, allowing them to witness the artistic process firsthand. Explore a diverse range of mediums, from painting and sculpture to ceramics and jewelry, and connect with the artists themselves as they share insights into their craft. This immersive experience offers a deeper understanding of the island's artistic landscape and fosters a sense of connection between artists and art enthusiasts.

The Whidbey Island Fair, a summertime tradition, brings together the island's agricultural heritage and community spirit. This multi-day event showcases livestock exhibits, 4-H demonstrations, live entertainment, and exhilarating carnival rides. Indulge in fair favorites like funnel cakes and cotton candy, cheer on participants in the rodeo, and immerse yourself in the lively atmosphere that permeates the fairgrounds. The Whidbey Island Fair is a celebration of community, creativity, and the island's rural roots.

For those with a passion for literature, the Whidbey Island Writers Conference is a must-attend event. Held annually, this gathering brings together aspiring writers, published authors, and industry professionals for workshops, panel discussions, and networking opportunities. Immerse yourself in the world of storytelling, learn from seasoned writers, and connect with fellow wordsmiths as you nourish your own creative journey.

Whidbey Island's holiday celebrations are filled with joy and enchantment. The Langley Tree Lighting Ceremony, held each December, transforms the town into a winter wonderland. Join the community as they gather to witness the lighting of the town's iconic Christmas tree, listen to carolers fill the air with melodious tunes, and sip on hot cocoa while strolling through the decorated streets. The spirit of the season is palpable as families come together to celebrate and create cherished memories.

Throughout the year, Whidbey Island's towns and communities host a variety of smaller-scale events that offer glimpses into the island's vibrant culture. From farmers markets and art walks to live music performances and theater productions, there is always something happening to captivate locals and visitors alike. Check the local event calendars and embrace the opportunity to immerse yourself in the island's spirited gatherings.

As you participate in Whidbey Island's events and festivals, allow yourself to be swept up in the contagious enthusiasm and sense of community that permeate the island. Engage with the locals, sample the flavors of the island's cuisine, and join in the festivities. These events are not only a celebration of Whidbey Island's rich traditions but also an invitation to connect with its welcoming and vibrant spirit.

As you reflect on your experiences at Whidbey Island's events and festivals, take a moment to appreciate the dedication and passion of the community members who work tirelessly to make these celebrations possible. Their commitment to preserving and sharing the island's culture and heritage creates a tapestry of vibrant experiences that enrich the lives of all who attend.

Chapter 13: Historical Legacies: Exploring Whidbey Island's Heritage

Whidbey Island is steeped in history, with a legacy that dates back centuries. In Chapter 13, we embark on a journey through time, exploring the island's rich historical heritage and uncovering the stories that have shaped Whidbey into the place it is today.

Ebey's Landing National Historical Reserve stands as a testament to the island's past, preserving the history of Whidbey's early settlers and their contributions to the development of the region. Take a walk along the bluff trail, which offers panoramic views of the prairie, Puget Sound, and the Olympic Mountains. Explore the historic buildings, such as the Jacob Ebey House and the Ferry House, which provide a glimpse into the island's pioneer era. Immerse yourself in the stories of the resilient individuals who settled the land, overcoming challenges and leaving a lasting legacy.

Coupeville, the second oldest town in Washington state, showcases a charming blend of historic architecture and maritime heritage. Stroll through the historic waterfront district, where beautifully preserved buildings house shops, galleries, and restaurants. Visit the Island County Historical Museum, which offers exhibits that delve into the island's history, from its Native American roots to its military presence during World War II. The Captain Thomas Coupe House and the Coupeville Wharf are other notable landmarks that speak to the town's historical significance.

Fort Casey Historical State Park takes visitors back in time to the era of coastal defense in the late 19th century. Explore the fort's well-preserved gun emplacements, wander through the barracks, and marvel at the iconic Admiralty Head Lighthouse. Learn about the strategic role the fort played in protecting the entrance to Puget Sound and its significance during times of conflict. The park's expansive grounds also offer opportunities for picnicking, beachcombing, and soaking in the natural beauty of the surroundings.

Langley, with its Victorian-era buildings and small-town charm, carries a historical legacy that is intertwined with the island's artistic and cultural heritage. Discover the history of the town at the South Whidbey Historical Museum, which offers exhibits on the region's early settlement, logging industry, and more. Langley's theater, housed in a historic building, showcases classic films and live performances, allowing visitors to experience the timeless charm of the town.

As you explore Whidbey Island's historical sites and landmarks, consider the intricate layers of human stories and the profound impact they have had on shaping the island's identity. Reflect on the struggles, triumphs, and everyday lives of those who came before, and appreciate their contributions to the vibrant community that exists today.

Whidbey Island's historical heritage is not limited to designated sites and buildings. It is embedded in the fabric of the island, woven into the stories and traditions of its residents. Engage with the local community, strike up conversations with islanders, and listen to their tales. They hold the living history of Whidbey, and through their words, you can gain a deeper understanding of the island's past and its continued evolution.

As you conclude your exploration of Whidbey Island's historical legacies, take a moment to honor the island's heritage and the importance of preserving its stories for future generations. The historical sites, museums, and the living memories of the island's residents ensure that the rich tapestry of Whidbey's history endures and continues to shape its future.

Chapter 14: Whidbey Island's Hidden Gems: Off the Beaten Path

While Whidbey Island is known for its popular attractions and well-known destinations, it also harbors a treasure trove of hidden gems tucked away off the beaten path. In Chapter 14, we venture beyond the tourist hotspots, uncovering the lesser-known but equally captivating corners of the island.

Located on the southern end of Whidbey Island, Possession Point State Park offers a serene escape from the bustling crowds. This hidden gem boasts a tranquil beach, shaded picnic areas, and picturesque views of the Olympic Mountains. Take a leisurely stroll along the shoreline, listening to the gentle lapping of the waves, or explore the park's forested trails that wind through lush greenery. Possession Point State Park offers a peaceful retreat where you can connect with nature and enjoy moments of solitude.

Nestled on the northeastern side of the island, Dugualla Bay Preserve presents a hidden oasis of natural beauty. This lesser-known gem offers walking trails that meander through scenic wetlands and forested areas, providing opportunities for birdwatching and wildlife spotting. Keep your eyes peeled for bald eagles soaring overhead, herons wading in the shallows, and deer grazing among the trees. Dugualla Bay

Preserve is a tranquil sanctuary where you can immerse yourself in the island's unspoiled landscapes.

For a taste of Whidbey Island's agricultural heritage, venture off the main roads and explore the island's rural countryside. The backroads of Central Whidbey are adorned with picturesque farms, vineyards, and orchards. Take a leisurely drive, stopping at farm stands along the way to purchase freshly harvested produce, homemade jams, or artisanal cheeses. Engage with the local farmers, learning about their sustainable practices and savoring the flavors of the island's agricultural bounty. The hidden agricultural gems of Whidbey Island offer a glimpse into the island's farming traditions and the vibrant community that sustains them.

Tucked away on the western side of the island, Admirals Cove Beach provides a secluded coastal retreat. This hidden gem offers a long stretch of sandy beach, perfect for long walks or quiet contemplation. Discover tide pools teeming with marine life, search for shells and sea glass, or simply relax on the shore while listening to the gentle rhythm of the waves. Admirals Cove Beach offers a serene escape from the crowds, allowing you to reconnect with the beauty and serenity of the island's coastline.

Further north, the charming community of Greenbank offers a delightful escape from the beaten path. Visit the

Greenbank Farm, a former loganberry farm turned community hub, where you can explore the fields, visit art galleries and shops, and indulge in freshly baked pies at the farm's famous café. Take a moment to savor the tranquility and natural beauty of the farm, and perhaps even catch a glimpse of the resident alpacas that graze in the fields. Greenbank's hidden charm offers a glimpse into the island's agricultural roots and the creativity of its residents.

As you venture off the beaten path and discover Whidbey Island's hidden gems, cherish the sense of exploration and the joy of uncovering treasures that are often overlooked. These lesser-known destinations reveal the quieter, more intimate side of the island, allowing you to forge a deeper connection with its landscapes, communities, and hidden stories.

Embrace the spirit of discovery, take the road less traveled, and allow yourself to be enchanted by the hidden gems that Whidbey Island has to offer. In these moments of solitude and serendipity, you may find the true essence of the island's enchantment.

Chapter 15: Reflections and Connections: Whidbey Island's Essence

As our journey on Whidbey Island nears its conclusion, Chapter 15 invites us to reflect on the experiences, connections, and the essence of this captivating island. Whidbey Island's essence is woven from the tapestry of its landscapes, communities, history, and the indelible memories created during our exploration.

Take a moment to pause and breathe in the island's salty air, feeling the gentle caress of the ocean breeze on your skin. Reflect on the natural beauty that surrounds you—the majestic forests, the sweeping shorelines, and the captivating sunsets that paint the sky in hues of gold and pink. Allow the tranquility of the island to seep into your soul, providing a sense of calm and connection with the world around you.

Whidbey Island's essence is also found in the warm and welcoming communities that call this place home. The genuine hospitality of its residents, their passion for the island's culture, and their commitment to preserving its treasures create a sense of belonging. Recall the conversations shared with locals, the stories they shared, and the connections made along the way. Whidbey Island's essence lies in the bonds forged and the friendships formed, leaving a lasting impression that extends beyond the boundaries of our journey.

Consider the island's rich history and heritage, the tales of early settlers, and the echoes of those who shaped the land. The whispers of the past can still be heard in the historic buildings, the preserved landmarks, and the stories passed down through generations. Whidbey Island's essence is interwoven with its historical legacies, reminding us of the resilience and spirit that have shaped the island's identity.

Whidbey Island's essence is a symphony of flavors, experienced through its culinary delights. Recall the tastes of farm-fresh produce, succulent seafood, and the nuanced notes of local wines. The island's commitment to sustainable practices and farm-to-table cuisine adds depth and richness to its culinary offerings. Whidbey Island's essence is found in the moments shared around the table, savoring the flavors and creating memories that linger long after the last bite.

As we conclude our exploration of Whidbey Island, let the essence of this remarkable place leave an imprint on your heart and mind. Carry the island's natural beauty, the warmth of its communities, and the stories of its past with you. Embrace the connections forged, the discoveries made, and the experiences that have enriched your journey.

Whidbey Island's essence is a tapestry of nature, culture, history, and human connections. It is a reminder of the beauty and wonder that can be found in our world, and a call to embrace the treasures that lie beyond our everyday routines. As you bid farewell to Whidbey Island, may its essence linger within you, inspiring a sense of curiosity, appreciation, and a longing to explore new horizons.

Remember that Whidbey Island will always welcome you back, ready to reveal new layers of its enchantment and invite you to create even more extraordinary chapters in your personal journey.

Chapter 16: Planning Your Whidbey Island Adventure

In Chapter 16, we shift our focus to planning your own Whidbey Island adventure. With the knowledge and inspiration gained from our exploration, it's time to craft your itinerary, consider practicalities, and embark on a personalized journey to this captivating island.

Choosing the Right Time: Whidbey Island has something to offer in every season. Consider the activities and events that interest you and align them with the island's calendar. From blooming wildflowers in spring to vibrant fall foliage, each season presents its own unique charm.

Mapping Your Route: Whidbey Island is easily accessible via ferry or bridge. Plan your route accordingly, taking into account your starting point and any desired stops along the way. Explore the island's towns, natural areas, and cultural landmarks to create a well-rounded itinerary.

Accommodations: Whidbey Island offers a range of accommodations to suit every preference. Choose from cozy bed and breakfasts, charming inns, vacation rentals, or campgrounds nestled in nature. Book your accommodations in advance to secure your preferred option.

Outdoor Adventures: Whidbey Island's natural beauty invites outdoor enthusiasts. Determine the activities that interest you, whether it's hiking, kayaking, beachcombing, or wildlife watching. Research the best trails, rental options, and guided tours to enhance your experience.

Cultural Exploration: Delve into the island's arts and culture scene by visiting galleries, attending performances, or participating in workshops. Check the event calendars for festivals, art walks, or live music performances during your visit.

Culinary Delights: Indulge in Whidbey Island's culinary offerings by visiting farmers markets, seafood restaurants, and local wineries. Discover the farm-to-table experiences, food festivals, and cooking classes that align with your interests.

Historical Discoveries: Immerse yourself in Whidbey Island's rich history by visiting historical sites, museums, and landmarks. Plan a visit to Ebey's Landing National Historical Reserve, the Island County Historical Museum, and other notable locations to deepen your understanding of the island's past.

Hidden Gems: Venture off the beaten path to uncover Whidbey Island's hidden gems. Research lesser-known beaches, nature reserves, or quaint communities that offer a sense of serenity and solitude.

Engaging with the Community: Connect with the locals by striking up conversations, attending community events, or engaging in workshops and classes. Embrace the island's welcoming spirit and learn from those who call Whidbey home.

Embracing Serendipity: While planning is important, leave room for spontaneity and unexpected discoveries. Allow yourself to wander, follow your instincts, and be open to the serendipitous moments that may enrich your Whidbey Island adventure.

Remember, your Whidbey Island journey is a personal one, shaped by your interests, preferences, and desire for exploration. Take the time to research, create a well-rounded itinerary, and immerse yourself in the island's natural beauty, cultural richness, and warm community spirit.

As you embark on your Whidbey Island adventure, cherish the moments, savor the flavors, and embrace the connections made along the way. Allow the island's enchantment to unfold before you, leaving a lasting impression and an indelible chapter in your own personal story.

Chapter 17: Sustainable Practices on Whidbey Island

In Chapter 17, we delve into the importance of sustainable practices on Whidbey Island and how visitors can contribute to preserving the island's natural beauty for future generations. As you plan your adventure, consider these sustainable guidelines to minimize your environmental impact and promote responsible tourism.

Respect the Natural Environment: Whidbey Island's pristine landscapes are fragile and deserve our utmost respect. Follow designated trails, avoid disturbing wildlife, and refrain from picking or damaging plants. Leave natural treasures untouched for others to enjoy.

Leave No Trace: Practice Leave No Trace principles by carrying out any waste you generate. Dispose of garbage and recyclables properly in designated containers. Leave the places you visit as pristine as you found them.

Support Local Businesses: Whidbey Island has a vibrant local economy. Support the community by shopping at local stores, dining at independent restaurants, and purchasing souvenirs from local artisans. This helps sustain the local economy and preserves the island's unique character.

Choose Sustainable Accommodations: Look for eco-friendly accommodations that prioritize sustainability. Consider staying at hotels or bed and breakfasts that implement energy-saving practices, waste reduction measures, and support local conservation efforts.

Opt for Sustainable Transportation: Consider eco-friendly transportation options such as cycling, walking, or using public transportation when exploring the island. If driving is necessary, carpool or rent hybrid or electric vehicles to minimize your carbon footprint.

Minimize Plastic Waste: Bring a reusable water bottle and refill it at designated water stations to reduce plastic waste. Avoid single-use plastics whenever possible and choose reusable or biodegradable alternatives.

Support Local Food: Explore the island's farm-to-table culture by dining at restaurants that prioritize locally sourced ingredients. Visit farmers markets to purchase fresh produce, supporting local farmers and reducing carbon emissions associated with long-distance food transport.

Conserve Water and Energy: Practice water and energy conservation by taking shorter showers, turning off lights and electronics when not in use, and adjusting thermostats to conserve energy. Respect the island's precious resources and use them responsibly.

Engage in Responsible Wildlife Viewing: When observing wildlife, maintain a safe distance and never disturb or feed animals. Follow wildlife watching guidelines and respect their habitats.

Learn and Educate: Take the opportunity to learn about the island's conservation efforts, environmental challenges, and initiatives. Share your knowledge with others, inspiring them to adopt sustainable practices as well.

By embracing sustainable practices, you can contribute to the preservation of Whidbey Island's natural beauty and help create a more sustainable future. Remember that small actions can make a significant difference in preserving this enchanting island for generations to come.

As you embark on your Whidbey Island adventure, let sustainability guide your choices, creating a positive impact and leaving a legacy of environmental stewardship. Together, we can ensure that the island's natural wonders endure for future visitors to enjoy.

Chapter 18: Capturing Whidbey Island: Photography Tips and Techniques

In Chapter 18, we explore the art of capturing Whidbey Island through photography. With its stunning landscapes, vibrant communities, and rich cultural heritage, Whidbey Island provides endless opportunities to create memorable and visually captivating photographs. Here are some tips and techniques to help you capture the essence of the island:

Plan and Research: Before setting out, research the island's iconic locations and hidden gems that you want to photograph. Check the weather forecast and consider the best time of day for capturing different scenes and lighting conditions.

Explore Different Perspectives: Experiment with different angles, vantage points, and compositions to create unique and interesting photographs. Get down low, climb up high, or try shooting from unexpected angles to add visual interest to your images.

Embrace Golden Hour: Take advantage of the magical light during the golden hours—the hour after sunrise and the hour before sunset. The warm, soft light during these times enhances the colors and textures of the landscapes, creating a magical atmosphere.

Capture Whidbey's Coastal Beauty: Whidbey Island is renowned for its picturesque coastline. Experiment with long exposures to create smooth, ethereal water effects, or capture the dramatic cliffs and rock formations that dot the shores. Incorporate elements such as driftwood, seashells, or crashing waves to add depth and interest to your coastal compositions.

Showcase Whidbey's Small-Town Charm: Whidbey Island's towns and communities offer captivating photo opportunities. Capture the unique architecture, charming streets, and vibrant local life. Engage with the residents, capturing candid moments that reflect the island's warm community spirit.

Focus on Nature's Details: Whidbey Island is a haven for nature enthusiasts. Zoom in on the intricate details of flora and fauna, capturing the delicate petals of wildflowers, the graceful flight of birds, or the textures of moss-covered trees. Macro photography can reveal the hidden beauty of the island's natural wonders.

Tell a Story: Use your photography to tell the story of your Whidbey Island adventure. Document the journey, capturing the moments, people, and experiences that define your trip. Incorporate elements of daily life, events, and cultural traditions to create a narrative that reflects the essence of the island.

Experiment with Long Exposures: Whidbey Island's landscapes lend themselves to long exposure photography. Use a tripod to capture the movement of clouds, create silky smooth water effects in waterfalls or coastal scenes, or capture the trails of stars during night photography.

Capture the Changing Seasons: Whidbey Island offers different visual delights throughout the seasons. From blooming wildflowers in spring to vibrant fall foliage, each season brings a unique color palette and atmosphere. Capture the island's seasonal transformations to showcase its natural beauty.

Edit with Care: Once you've captured your images, take the time to enhance them through post-processing. Use editing software to adjust colors, contrast, and sharpness while maintaining the natural beauty of the scenes. Be mindful not to over-edit and preserve the authentic essence of your Whidbey Island photographs.

Remember to enjoy the process of capturing Whidbey Island through your lens. Embrace the island's beauty, immerse yourself in its culture, and allow your creativity to shine through your photographs. By capturing the essence of Whidbey Island, you can share its magic with others and create lasting visual memories of your adventure.

Chapter 19: Whidbey Island's Literary Connection

In Chapter 19, we explore the literary connection of Whidbey Island, delving into the island's influence on writers, its vibrant literary community, and the ways in which literature has shaped the island's identity.

Literary Inspiration: Whidbey Island's natural beauty, rich history, and vibrant community have long been a source of inspiration for writers. The island's landscapes, from the rugged coastlines to the serene forests, provide a captivating backdrop for storytelling. Explore the works of authors who have been inspired by Whidbey Island, such as Sarah Orne Jewett, who set her novel "The Country of the Pointed Firs" on the island.

Whidbey Island Writers Conference: The Whidbey Island Writers Conference is an annual event that attracts both established and emerging writers. Attend workshops, panel discussions, and readings to engage with the literary community, learn from experienced authors, and nurture your own writing journey.

Independent Bookstores: Whidbey Island is home to several independent bookstores that showcase a curated selection of books, including works by local authors. Visit these bookstores to browse through their collections, attend author readings, and connect with fellow book lovers. Some notable bookstores on the island include Moonraker Books in Langley and Kingfisher Books in Coupeville.

Writing Workshops and Groups: Whidbey Island offers opportunities for writers to refine their craft and connect with like-minded individuals. Join writing workshops or writing groups to receive feedback on your work, share ideas, and be part of a supportive writing community. Engage in creative writing exercises that are inspired by the island's landscapes, people, and history.

Literary Events and Readings: Keep an eye out for literary events and readings happening on the island. Authors, poets, and storytellers often visit Whidbey Island to share their work with the community. Attend these events to listen to readings, engage in discussions, and celebrate the power of words.

Whidbey Island Literary Festival: The Whidbey Island Literary Festival is a biennial event that celebrates literature and storytelling. Featuring author panels, book signings, and interactive sessions, this festival brings together readers, writers, and literary enthusiasts. Immerse yourself in the literary world and discover new voices and perspectives.

Book Clubs: Whidbey Island has a vibrant book club community where readers gather to discuss books, share insights, and foster a love of literature. Join a book club to engage in thought-provoking discussions and connect with fellow bookworms.

Writing Retreats: Consider participating in a writing retreat on Whidbey Island. These retreats provide dedicated time and space for writers to focus on their craft, surrounded by the island's inspiring landscapes. Disconnect from distractions and immerse yourself in a nurturing environment that encourages creativity and reflection.

Poetry and Storytelling Events: Whidbey Island hosts poetry readings and storytelling events that celebrate the spoken word. Engage with the island's vibrant literary community by attending these events, sharing your own work, or simply listening to the captivating performances.

Writing in Nature: Whidbey Island's natural landscapes offer tranquil settings for writers seeking inspiration. Find a peaceful spot on the beach, in a forest, or near a tranquil lake to connect with nature and let the words flow. Use the island's beauty as a backdrop for your writing, allowing the essence of Whidbey to infuse your words.

Whidbey Island's literary connection is a testament to the island's ability to nurture creativity, ignite imaginations, and provide a sanctuary for writers. Immerse yourself in the island's literary offerings, engage with the community, and let the power of words intertwine with the spirit of Whidbey Island.

Chapter 20: Whidbey Island's Endless Discoveries

In Chapter 20, we conclude our exploration of Whidbey Island by embracing the idea that the island's treasures are never-ending. Whidbey Island offers endless discoveries for those willing to delve deeper into its landscapes, communities, and hidden corners.

Embrace Serendipity: As you continue to explore Whidbey Island, remain open to serendipitous moments and unexpected discoveries. Allow yourself to wander off the beaten path, follow your instincts, and let the island unveil its secrets at its own pace.

Return Again and Again: Whidbey Island's allure is such that a single visit may not be enough to truly uncover all its wonders. Consider making Whidbey Island a place of return, where each visit offers new experiences, deepens connections, and strengthens your bond with the island.

Engage with the Community: Whidbey Island's vibrant and welcoming community is an endless source of connection and enrichment. Engage with the locals, strike up conversations, attend community events, and become a part of the island's tapestry of stories and experiences.

Preserve and Protect: As you continue to explore Whidbey Island, remember the importance of preserving and protecting its natural beauty and cultural heritage. Leave no trace, support local conservation efforts, and promote sustainable practices that ensure the island's treasures endure for generations to come.

Share Your Whidbey Story: Whidbey Island has a way of leaving a lasting impact on those who visit. Share your Whidbey story with others, whether through photographs, writing, or personal anecdotes. Inspire others to discover and connect with this enchanting island.

Inspire Curiosity: Whidbey Island's endless discoveries serve as an invitation to embrace curiosity and a spirit of exploration. Encourage others to embark on their own Whidbey adventures, sparking their curiosity and igniting their desire to uncover the island's hidden gems.

Carry Whidbey in Your Heart: Even when you're away from Whidbey Island, carry its essence in your heart. Allow the island's beauty, stories, and memories to continue inspiring you, fostering a sense of connection and appreciation for the special place that is Whidbey.

Whidbey Island's endless discoveries extend beyond the boundaries of this book. Embrace the joy of continued exploration, allowing Whidbey Island to weave its magic into the fabric of your life. With each visit, each encounter, and each new chapter in your Whidbey journey, the island's enchantment will continue to unfold, offering an everlasting source of inspiration and wonder.

As we bid farewell to Whidbey Island, remember that its treasures are forever imprinted in your memories. Carry the spirit of the island with you as you venture forth, and may the lessons learned, the connections made, and the experiences cherished on Whidbey Island guide you on your future explorations.

Made in United States
Troutdale, OR
05/26/2024